Reader's Guides

SECOND SERIES III

BRITISH
THEATRE HISTORY

by

ALEC CLUNES

T0343554

PUBLISHED FOR

THE NATIONAL BOOK LEAGUE

AT THE UNIVERSITY PRESS

CAMBRIDGE

1955

CAMBRIDGE
UNIVERSITY PRESS

University Printing House, Cambridge CB2 8BS, United Kingdom

Cambridge University Press is part of the University of Cambridge.

It furthers the University's mission by disseminating knowledge in the pursuit of
education, learning and research at the highest international levels of excellence.

www.cambridge.org
Information on this title: www.cambridge.org/9781107475151

© Cambridge University Press 1955

First published 1955
First paperback edition 2014

A catalogue record for this publication is available from the British Library

ISBN 978-1-107-47515-1 Paperback

Contents

Introduction

THE theatre is a slippery affair, and that means, according to the dictionary, that it is elusive, evasive, apt to slip, unstable and uncertain. It can have other qualities too— glamour, for instance, in both its senses ("enchantment" and "studied charm"), and dignity and warmth and certainly nostalgia. Of these, and they are but a few of the attributes that go to make up so complex an organism, it is nostalgia that is responsible for many of the books that have been written about the theatre. The actor writes of his successes, the historian seeks to recreate the past, and both are hampered by the fact that the theatre is slippery.

Now whereas a film can be taken out of its tin and projected, (and after a decade or two it will look very different from our recollection of it), a theatrical performance has only memory, which can be very treacherous, and contemporary record, which can be inadequate or prejudiced, for its recreation. Not many of us will follow the example of an eminent writer who keeps a notebook on his knee when he visits the theatre in order to make an immediate record of any memorable moment, so that he will know, when the knowledge is needed, exactly what happened when, for instance, Sir Laurence Olivier turned himself into a puff of wind as Justice Shallow and floated off the stage. Even then there is a strong chance that Sir Laurence's technique was so many steps ahead of the eye, let alone the pencil, that our writer will know no more than we do after ten years, which is that in some elusive, slippery way Justice Shallow was gone with the wind.

Well, there it is. People do like to recall what the Gielguds and Oliviers of our time, and the Garricks and Keans of past time, did, and by a simple extension what sort of people they are and were, so that in the event more perhaps gets written about Kean's adventures with his lady friend, "Little Breeches", than about the way in which he tackled the part of Hamlet, not because we are more interested in amours than in acting, but because it is so much easier, the theatre being elusive and slippery, to write that way.

It must at the same time be remembered that we live in a scientific age, and that even the evasive nostalgia of the theatre can be subject to a certain degree of precise reconstruction. Dr. Leslie Hotson will search through the uttermost dusty cellar of the Records Office, will search Europe if necessary, to piece together all the shreds of evidence that enable him to write a long and exciting book on the first performance of *Twelfth Night*. Mr. Richard Southern will hear of a derelict old theatre at the other end of the kingdom and he will measure every brick and examine every cranny until he can tell us, more precisely than we have known before, just what were the conditions under which an actor of a particular period performed.

This modern approach to research does mean that, although there will always be the incorrigible writer on the theatre who will use his uncertain memory and his scissoring and pasting of his predecessors' errors, there is at long last some chance that there will be an ever-increasing proportion of books that will, behind the aura of nostalgia, (and when nostalgia disappears let there be no more books about the theatre, for they will be dead, cold things), have a background of patiently collected fact. We must be grateful in this connection for the splendid pioneer work of the late W. J. Lawrence, who, in a lifetime of theatrical research, delved into every corner of our theatrical past. He did much to establish a standard that has made possible an exceptional study such as Dr. Hillebrand's *Kean* and the important contributions of Dr. Sprague to the history of Shakespearian acting—*Shakespeare and the Actors* and *Shakespearian Players and Performances*.

With the cheering thought that the attitude towards writing about the theatre is, on the whole, much improved, let us return to the problems that still face the writer, and particularly to the problem of how to write about acting. Mr. Haskell, in his introduction to *Ballet*, in the first series of NBL *Reader's Guides*, complained that "the writer on the ballet is more handicapped than the writer on any other art form, in that he cannot use quotations". Well, it is true that the writer on the theatre can inform you that Edwin Forrest used to maltreat the punctuation when playing Shakespeare, and quote examples to prove it, but all that will tell you is that Forrest was rather stupid and made innovations of no value. It will not tell you how he acted. Even precise contemporary descriptions, rare as they are, will not tell the whole story. Take for instance Lichtenberg's famous description of Garrick's Hamlet at his meeting with the Ghost: "Garrick turns sharply and at the same moment staggers back two or three paces with his knees giving way under him: his hat falls to the ground and both his arms, especially the left, are stretched out nearly to their full length, with the hands as high as his head, the right arm more bent and the hand lower, and the fingers apart; his mouth is open".*

Taken by itself this might merely give us the idea that Garrick's acting was very mannered and exaggerated. But put that description side by side with Partridge's remark in *Tom Jones*, "I am sure if I had seen a Ghost, I should have looked in the very same Manner, and done just what he did",

---

*(*Lichtenberg's Visits to England as described in his Letters and Diaries*, translated and annotated by Margaret L. Mare and W. H. Quarrell. Oxford, Clarendon Press, 1938.)

and we are reminded that, to the eighteenth-century eye, Garrick was acting with exceptional realism. Only the handful of really great actors can, of course, command anything like enough of this sort of detailed description for a complete impression of the actor as actor to emerge. Every little scrap of information must be pieced together in the hope that a recognisable whole may be achieved.

That is the principle on which any book on the past of the theatre should be written, whether it is a general history or about a particular theatre or actor. When it comes to dealing with the contemporary theatre, the facts may be easier to establish, but the assessment of the facts may be even more difficult to accomplish. The majority of the books on the theatre of today are written by professional critics, but no two critics will see the theatre with the same eye. Each is subject to his own general outlook and also to his own particular quirks. Suppose, for example, that a distinguished actor appears in a rather slight new play. One critic will say that he is wasting his time appearing in such flimsy nonsense, another that he has achieved wonders with unpromising material, another that the play is just as delightful as the actor's performance, another that the play will run for years (a statement that sometimes makes it very difficult to tell whether the critic thinks that the play is extremely good or extremely bad). Who can say which of these judgments is the right one? The important thing is that the opinion, whatever it is, shall be an honest expression of personal reaction based on experience.

Read, then, as widely as you can about the contemporary theatre, so that you can balance one opinion against another, and, best of all, broaden your experience of the theatre and develop your own critical faculties by going to it as often as you can. Such a course will have the double advantage of benefiting the theatre as well as yourself.

A word about the list of books which follows. It is concerned with the theatre, that is to say with the actual performance of dramatic works rather than the works themselves. The play as a form of literature has already been dealt with in earlier NBL lists, *British Drama* (1950, 1s.) and *Shakespeare* (1952, 1s. 6d.), to which this Reader's Guide is, up to a point, complementary. Mercifully, however, it is not now the custom to regard a play as something that can be divorced from the reality of performance and studied merely as a piece of printed literature. There is therefore inevitably some overlapping between this list and the previous ones, accompanied by some deviation of purpose.

The present list is intended for the ordinary reader. It does not exclude scholarly works, but it does omit many important books that are not in the ordinary sense readable. It does not, for example, include the Reverend John Genest's *Some Account of the English Stage, from the Restoration in* 1660 *to* 1830 (Bath, 1832), which is still regarded as a basic history of our theatre, but whose ten volumes consist largely of transcriptions of details from thousands of playbills. It is the offspring of great industry and great enthusiasm, but it is not a book with which to curl up in a fireside chair.

One of the great advantages of contemporary books of non-fiction is that often they give lists of other books on the same subject. By this means the reader can be enticed into a range much larger than is represented here.

As an example whither we may be led, let us take one of the books at random from our list—Whitworth's *The Making of a National Theatre*. This has a quite short bibliography of seven items, but they include two of Granville-Barker's most important books, not listed here, *The National Theatre* and *The Exemplary Theatre*. The former gives detailed plans for a scheme that may well bear fruit, should our country continue to be prosperous, in the very near future. The latter is a

9

classic analysis of what the theatre does and what it ought to do. You will also find a reference in Mr. Whitworth's list to *Drama*, the organ of the British Drama League, the catalogue of whose library is given among our reference books. *Drama*, should you subscribe to it, will serve the excellent purpose of bringing to your notice all the books of any consequence on the theatre that are in current publication, and will enable you to keep this present list up-to-date.

If you should, in the course of time, become completely fascinated by theatre books, you would be well advised to invest half-a-crown in Mr. I. Kyrle Fletcher's catalogue of the National Book League's exhibition on the British Theatre (Cambridge University Press, 1950). This will lead you into a new world of theatre books, rare and exotic. At the same time you should join the Society for Theatre Research (103, Ralph Court, Queensway, London, W2). If you live within reach of London you can attend the Society's lectures and, wherever you live, you will receive an admirable quarterly called *Theatre Notebook*.

Whether you skim the new books or venture into the antiquarian undergrowth, good luck in your reading. You will be unlikely to find a more fascinating subject.

Reading List

This list has been compiled by Bertram Shuttleworth, in consultation with Alec Clunes. Some of the books are out-of-print, but if they cannot be bought either new or secondhand, most of them can be found in libraries. All publishers are London firms, except where otherwise stated. So far as possible dates of the latest editions are given. Prices (net and subject to alteration) are given only where a book is known to be available new at the time this list goes to press.

HISTORY

General

DISHER, M. WILLSON. *Pleasures of London*. Hale, 1950.

Covers many minor places of entertainment that do not find their way into more general histories.

HOBSON, HAROLD. *Theatre*. Burke, 1953. 21s.

An anthology, with commentary, under the headings: The Audience; Actors and Actresses; Great Moments; Mishaps and Excitements; Controversy; Emotion.

MARRIOTT, J. W. *The Theatre*. Harrap, 1945. 8s. 6d.

Intended for "the young man or woman who enjoys the theatre and would rather like a few hints about drama and theatre-going".

NAGLER, A. M. (Editor). *Sources of Theatrical History*. New York, Theatre Annual; London, C. & I. K. Fletcher, 1952. 52s. 6d.

A comprehensive and useful anthology.

NICOLL, ALLARDYCE. *The Development of the Theatre: A Study of Theatrical Art from the Beginnings to the Present Day*. Harrap, 3rd edition, 1948. 36s.

A standard history with 315 illustrations. Several chapters deal with the British theatre.

11

The English Theatre: A Short History. Nelson, 1936.
Concise, and with a useful list of London theatres.

A History of English Drama, 1660–1900: I, *Restoration Drama*, 1660–1700; II, *Early Eighteenth-Century Drama*, 1700–1750; III, *Late Eighteenth-Century Drama*, 1750–1800; IV, *Early Nineteenth-Century Drama*, 1800–1850; V, Parts I and II, *Late Nineteenth-Century Drama*, 1850–1900. Cambridge University Press, revised editions, Vols. I–III, 1952, each 35s.; Vol. IV, 1955 *(forthcoming)*; Vol. V, 1946, Part I, 25s., Part II, 50s. new edition *in preparation*.

Mostly concerned with drama but each period includes a chapter on the theatre and there are useful handlists of plays with the places and dates of first performances.

WILSON, A. E. *East End Entertainment.* Barker, 1954. 30s.

Many important theatres have been located in the East End of London, from Shakespeare's time up to the rebuilding of the People's Palace in 1936.

Chronological

CHAMBERS, Sir E. K. *The Mediaeval Stage.* Oxford, Clarendon Press, 1903. 2 vols. 63s.

The Elizabethan Stage. Oxford, Clarendon Press, 1923. 4 vols. 126s.

Two works of exceptional scholarship, for reference rather than for reading.

LAWRENCE, WILLIAM J. *Pre-Restoration Stage Studies.* Harvard University Press; Oxford University Press, 1927.

The latest of Lawrence's books to remain in print, but any of this writer's work is of importance. He did much pioneer research on the *minutiae* of stage history.

HODGES, C. WALTER. *The Globe Restored: A Study of the Elizabethan Theatre.* Benn, 1953. 50s.

Very well illustrated, not least by the author's own drawings.

BENTLEY, GERALD EADES. *The Jacobean and Caroline Stage: Dramatic Companies and Players*. Oxford, Clarendon Press, 1941. 2 volumes. 84s.

A continuation of Sir E. K. Chambers's work.

HOTSON, LESLIE. *The Commonwealth and Restoration Stage*. Harvard University Press; Oxford University Press, 1928.

A study of surreptitious drama, 1642–55, and of playhouses and companies, 1655–1704.

DOWNES, JOHN (ed. Montague Summers). *Roscius Anglicanus*. Fortune Press (1928). 42s.

A contemporary record of the Restoration stage.

SUMMERS, MONTAGUE. *The Restoration Theatre*. Kegan Paul, 1934.

A study of staging.

ROSENFELD, SYBIL. *Strolling Players and Drama in the Provinces, 1660–1765*. Cambridge University Press, 1939.

MANDER, RAYMOND and JOE MITCHENSON, *Hamlet Through the Ages: A Pictorial Record from 1709*. Rockliff, 1952. 35s.

WATSON, ERNEST BRADLEE. *Sheridan to Robertson: A Study of the Nineteenth-Century London Stage*. Harvard University Press; Oxford University Press, 1926.

The most important study of a neglected period.

SOUTHERN, RICHARD. *The Georgian Playhouse*. Pleiades, 1948. 12s. 6d.

Based on practical examination of existing theatres.

BADDELEY, V. C. CLINTON-. *All Right on the Night*. Putnam, 1954. 21s.

Slight but attractive studies of the Georgian theatre and pantomime.

HUDSON, LYNTON. *The English Stage, 1850–1950*. Harrap, 1951. 10s. 6d.

BAILY, LESLIE. *The Gilbert and Sullivan Book*. Cassell, 1952. 42s.

Contains over 400 illustrations, all equally fascinating if not all equally relevant.

SPEAIGHT, ROBERT. *William Poel and the Elizabethan Revival.* Heinemann, 1954. 21s.

Poel was a pioneer advocate of a return to Elizabethan staging.

ST. JOHN, CHRISTOPHER (Editor). *Ellen Terry and Bernard Shaw: A Correspondence.* Reinhardt, 1949. 25s.

The secret history of the struggle between the old world of Irving and the new world of Shaw.

MANDER, RAYMOND and JOE MITCHENSON. *Theatrical Companion to Shaw: A Pictorial Record of the First Performances of the Plays of George Bernard Shaw.* Rockliff, 1955. 42s.

A much more exhaustive survey of the Shavian scene than the sub-title would suggest.

WILSON, A. E. *Edwardian Theatre.* Barker, 1951. 21s.

POGSON, REX. *Miss Horniman and the Gaiety Theatre, Manchester.* Rockliff, 1952. 21s.

Miss Horniman, who also founded the Abbey Theatre, Dublin, was as great a revolutionary in her day as Shaw.

WHITWORTH, GEOFFREY. *The Making of a National Theatre.* Faber, 1951. 25s.

The story of a persistent struggle for the establishment of a British National Theatre.

LANDSTONE, CHARLES. *Off-Stage: A Personal Record of the First Twelve Years of State Sponsored Drama in Great Britain.* Elek, 1953. 18s.

The history of C.E.M.A. and the Arts Council.

MARSHALL, NORMAN. *The Other Theatre.* Lehmann, 1947. 15s.

An oustanding book on the non-commercial theatre. Not to be missed.

WILLIAMSON, AUDREY. *Theatre of Two Decades.* Rockliff, 1951. 12s. 6d.

The London theatre of the nineteen-thirties and forties.

TREWIN, J. C. (Editor). *Theatre Programme.* Muller, 1954. 15s.

Fifteen essays, mostly by leading critics, on the contemporary theatre.

14

Individual Theatres

Birmingham Repertory

KEMP, THOMAS C. *Birmingham Repertory Theatre: The Playhouse and the Man*. Birmingham, Cornish, 1948. 15s.

The Birmingham Repertory theatre is the *nom de théatre* of Sir Barry Jackson, a great patron and amateur (in the finest sense of the word), who has devoted his life to the good of the theatre.

Court

MACCARTHY, Sir DESMOND. *The Court Theatre* 1904–1907: *A Commentary and Criticism*. Bullen, 1907.

With Vedrenne at the Court Theatre and later with Frohman at the Duke of York's, Granville-Barker directed outstanding seasons on National Theatre lines.

Covent Garden

WYNDHAM, HENRY SAXE. *The Annals of Covent Garden Theatre from* 1732 *to* 1897. Chatto, 1906. 2 vols.

Drury Lane

POPE, W. MACQUEEN. *Theatre Royal, Drury Lane*. Allen, 1951.

Mr. Macqueen Pope's historical surveys are erratic but racy.

Dublin

MACLIAMMÓIR, MICHEÁL. *All for Hecuba: An Irish Theatrical Autobiography*. Methuen, 1946.

Records the story of Dublin's Gate Theatre. Exceptionally entertaining.

ROBINSON, LENNOX. *Ireland's Abbey Theatre: A History*, 1899–1951. Sidgwick, 1951. 30s.

The Abbey Theatre has functioned as an Irish National Theatre in a way that has no parallel in recent English theatrical history.

Haymarket

POPE, W. MACQUEEN. *Haymarket: Theatre of Perfection*. Allen, 1948.

Lyceum

WILSON, A. E. *The Lyceum.* Yates, 1952. 18s.

See also, if possible, Austin Brereton's *The Lyceum and Henry Irving* (Lawrence & Bullen, 1903), for its excellent illustrations.

Lyric, Hammersmith

PLAYFAIR, SIR NIGEL. *The Story of the Lyric Theatre, Hammersmith.* Chatto, 1925.

In the twenties the devotee went to Barnes to see Tchekhov, but all London went to Hammersmith to see *The Beggar's Opera.*

Manchester, Gaiety

See Pogson, Rex, p. 14.

Old Vic and Sadler's Wells

DENT, EDWARD J. *A Theatre for Everybody: The Story of the Old Vic and Sadler's Wells.* Boardman, 1945.

WILLIAMSON, AUDREY. *Old Vic Drama: A Twelve Years' Study of Plays and Players.* Rockliff, 1948. 15s.

Stratford-upon-Avon

KEMP, THOMAS C., and TREWIN, J. C. *The Stratford Festival: A History of the Shakespeare Memorial Theatre.* Birmingham, Cornish, 1953. 25s.

See also BENSON, Sir FRANK, p. 17.

BIOGRAPHY

The field of theatrical biography is so enormous that the following cannot hope to be more than an arbitrary selection. A few are important, some are merely readable. For an extensive handlist, see the latest edition of *Who's Who in the Theatre.*

Edward Alleyn (1566–1626)

HOSKING, G. L. *The Life and Times of Edward Alleyn, Actor, Master of the King's Bears, Founder of the College of God's Gift at Dulwich, with a brief account of the Foundation up to its remodelling in 1857 and a Note on the Picture Gallery.* Cape, 1952. 15s.

More information has been preserved about Alleyn than about

Burbage, of whom there is, unfortunately, no similar biography, although both actors were equally important in the Elizabethan theatre, with Burbage having the advantage of creating most of the great Shakespearean roles.

Harley Granville-Barker (1877–1946)

PURDOM, C. B. *Granville-Barker*. Rockliff, 1955 (*forthcoming*). About 30s.

Sir Frank Benson (1858–1939)

BENSON, Sir FRANK. *My Memoirs*. Benn, 1930.

The influence of Benson's long association with the early Stratford Festivals and the number of outstanding actors who were nurtured in his company has not yet been adequately assessed. *See also* Lady Benson's *Mainly Players* (Thornton Butterworth, 1926).

Colley Cibber (1671–1757)

CIBBER, COLLEY. *An Apology for the Life of Mr. Colley Cibber*.

First published 1740. Various later publishers; the handiest edition is in Everyman's Library (Dent). The only English theatrical autobiography than can claim to have become a classic, this also provides the best account of the late Restoration and early eighteenth-century stage.

Sir Charles B. Cochran (1872–1951)

COCHRAN, Sir CHARLES. *The Secrets of a Showman*. Heinemann, 1925.

The best of several autobiographical books by this remarkable producer.

Noel Coward

COWARD, NOEL. *Present Indicative*. Heinemann, 1950. 12s. 6d.

Equally brilliant as actor, writer and composer, Coward belongs essentially to the restless period between the wars.

Dame Edith Evans

TREWIN, J. C. *Edith Evans*. Rockliff, 1954. 12s. 6d.

Includes a list of Dame Edith's performances, with over seventy illustrations.

David Garrick (1717–1779)

BARTON, MARGARET. *Garrick*. Faber, 1948.

The only recent biography and a very pleasantly written one, with a useful bibliography.

Sir John Gielgud

GIELGUD, Sir JOHN. *Early Stages*. Falcon Press, 1949. 12s. 6d.

Sir John Gielgud's autobiography up to 1936, with illustrations of later performances and a list of his appearances to 1948.

Sir John Martin-Harvey (1863–1944)

HARVEY, Sir JOHN MARTIN-. *Autobiography*. Sampson Low, 1933.

Includes many reminiscences of Irving. It must not be forgotten that Martin-Harvey performed such plays as *Oedipus Rex*, in association with Reinhardt, and *Pelleas and Melisande*, as well as *The Only Way*.

Sir Henry Irving (1838–1905)

IRVING, LAURENCE. *Henry Irving: The Actor and his World*. Faber, 1951. 50s.

The latest and most thorough, as well as the most objective, biography; by the actor's grandson.

CRAIG, EDWARD GORDON. *Henry Irving*. Dent, 1930.

By Ellen Terry's son, himself an outstanding figure in the history of the theatre. As a young man he was a member of Irving's company and he gives a personal and very interesting view.

Edmund Kean (1787–1833)

HILLEBRAND, HAROLD NEWCOMB. *Edmund Kean*. Columbia University Press; Oxford University Press, 1933.

The best of modern theatrical biographies. Difficult to come by but well worth chasing.

PLAYFAIR, GILES. *Kean: The Life and Paradox of the Great Actor*. Reinhardt, 1950. 12s. 6d.

The next best if Hillebrand is not obtainable.

Roger Kemble (1721–1802) and family

TREWIN, J. C. *The Kembles*. Werner Laurie (Shorter Lives Series), 1955 (*forthcoming*). 10s. 6d.

A brief introduction to this family of players.

John Philip Kemble (1757–1823)

BAKER, HERSCHEL. *John Philip Kemble: The Actor in his Theatre.* Harvard University Press; Oxford University Press, 1942. 32s.

The only full-scale modern study of an actor who has been undeservedly overshadowed by his sister, Mrs. Siddons.

William Charles Macready (1793–1873)

TOYNBEE, WILLIAM (Editor). *The Diaries of William Charles Macready*, 1833–1851. Chapman and Hall, 1912. 2 volumes.

This is probably the most revealing as well as the most extensive of theatrical autobiographies.

TREWIN, J. C. *Mr. Macready*. Harrap, 1955 (?July). About 15s.

A definitive biography of Macready by Alan S. Downer is forthcoming.

Sir Laurence and Lady Olivier (Vivien Leigh)

BARKER, FELIX. *The Oliviers*. Hamish Hamilton, 1953. 15s.

William Shakespeare (1564–1616)

BROWN, IVOR. *Shakespeare*. Collins, 1949.

CHUTE, MARCHETTE. *Shakespeare of London*. Secker, 1951. 15s.

These two biographies present, in popular form, many of the findings of recent scholarship. Both are eminently readable. For a more comprehensive bibliography (Miss Chute gives eight pages) see the National Book League Book List, *Shakespeare* (1952, 1s. 6d.).

Richard Brinsley Sheridan (1751–1816)

GIBBS, LEWIS. *Sheridan*. Dent, 1947.

Apart from his brief brilliance as a dramatist, Sheridan's chief claim to theatrical fame was that, as Manager of Drury Lane, he undid much of the good achieved by Garrick. He caused theatres to be impossibly large and actors to be impossibly poor.

19

George Bernard Shaw (1856–1950)

PEARSON, HESKETH. *Bernard Shaw: His Life and Personality.* Collins, 1950.

Sarah Siddons (1755–1831)

FFRENCH, YVONNE. *Mrs Siddons: Tragic Actress.* Deutsch, 1954. 21s.

A revised edition of a well-written biography of the one English actress who may certainly claim greatness. No index.

Dame Ellen Terry (1847–1928)

TERRY, DAME ELLEN. *Ellen Terry's Memoirs, with Preface, Notes and Additional Biographical Chapters by Edith Craig and Christopher St. John.* Gollancz, 1933.

Dame Sybil Thorndike

THORNDIKE, RUSSELL. *Sybil Thorndike.* Rockliff, 1950.

Dame Sybil has been very fortunate in having a brother who is a professional writer as well as actor. The first half of this book might well be called "The making of an actress".

Sir Herbert Beerbohm Tree (1853–1917)

BEERBOHM, MAX (Editor). *Herbert Beerbohm Tree: Some Memories of Him and of his Art.* Hutchinson, (1920).

A memorial tribute with a long memoir by Lady Tree and contributions by Bernard Shaw, Max Beerbohm and others.

Collective

RUSSELL, W. CLARK. *Representative Actors.* Warne, first published 1872.

So often reprinted that it should not be difficult to obtain secondhand. A valuable selection of snippets from many sources on every important actor from Alleyn to Toole.

PEARSON, HESKETH. *The Last Actor-Managers.* Methuen, 1950. 18s.

Forbes-Robertson, Tree, Alexander, Benson, Waller, Martin-Harvey, H.B. and Laurence Irving, Asche, Granville-Barker.

CRITICISM

AGATE, JAMES. *Brief Chronicles: A Survey of the Plays of Shakespeare and the Elizabethans in Actual Performance*. Cape, 1943.

Red Letter Nights: A Survey of the Post-Elizabethan Drama in Actual Performance on the London Stage, 1921–1943. Cape, 1944.

Immoment Toys: A Survey of Light Entertainment on the London Stage, 1920–1943. Cape, 1945.

BEERBOHM, MAX. *Around Theatres*. Hart-Davis, 1953. 30s.

A selection of Beerbohm's criticisms contributed to the *Saturday Review*, 1898–1910.

FARJEON, HERBERT. *The Shakespearean Scene: Dramatic Criticisms*. Hutchinson, 1949.

The period covered is 1913–44.

HAZLITT, WILLIAM (ed. William Archer and Robert W. Lowe). *Dramatic Essays*. Walter Scott, 1895. Now available only in *Complete Works*, Dent, £16 16s.

First published as *A View of the English Stage*, 1818. That Hazlitt was a critic when Kean was an actor may be regarded as a major blessing to our theatrical literature.

HUNT, LEIGH (ed. Lawrence Huston Houtchens and Carolyn Washburn Houtchens). *Leigh Hunt's Dramatic Criticism*, 1808–1831. Oxford University Press, 1950. 36s.

MACCARTHY, Sir DESMOND. *Theatre*. Macgibbon, 1954. 12s. 6d.

Criticisms mostly contributed to *The New Statesman*, 1914–1944.

MONTAGUE, C. E. *Dramatic Values*. Chatto, 1910.

Mostly contributed to *The Manchester Guardian*.

SHAW, GEORGE BERNARD. *Our Theatres in the Nineties*. Constable, 3 volumes, 7s. 6d. each.

A classic "must" of dramatic criticism. If you can bear to have less than the whole there is a selection, *Plays and Players*, Oxford University Press (World's Classics). 5s.

TYNAN, KENNETH. *He that Plays the King: A View of the Theatre.* Longmans, 1950.

The first flowering of our most promising young critic.

WARD, A. C. (Editor). *Specimens of English Dramatic Criticism, Seventeenth to Twentieth Centuries.* Oxford University Press (World's Classics). 5s.

From Samuel Pepys to Alan Dent.

TECHNIQUE

This section deals only with the history and development of theatre techniques; for a list of practical manuals the reader is recommended to refer to the Library Association's Guide, *Stagecraft and the Theatre* (1952, 6d.).

BARKER, HARLEY GRANVILLE-. *Prefaces to Shakespeare.* Sidgwick & Jackson, 5 volumes, 1927–48. Vol. 1, 2, 4, 5, 16s. each; Vol. 3, 17s. 6d.

The five series of these *Prefaces* represent the highly intellectual approach of one of the most outstanding English men of the theatre towards the performance of ten of the Shakespeare plays.

COLE, TOBY and HELEN KRICH CHINOY (Editors). *Actors on Acting: The Theories, Techniques and Practices of the Great Actors of All Times as told in their Own Words.* Pitman, 1952, 40s.

Directing the Play: A Source Book of Stagecraft. P. Owen and Vision Press, 1954, 42s.

A short history of production, with essays and working notes by famous producers.

CRAIG, GORDON. *On the Art of the Theatre.* Heinemann. First published 1911.

A book which has had perhaps more influence than any other on modern ideas of staging and production.

CRAUFORD, LANE. *Acting: Its Theory and Practice, with Illustrative Examples of Players Past and Present.* Constable, 1930.

DARLINGTON, W. A. *The Actor and his Audience.* Phoenix, 1949.

A history of English acting from a viewpoint rather different from that of Dr. Sprague (see below).

22

DAVIES, W. ROBERTSON. *Shakespeare's Boy Actors*. Dent, 1939.

An assessment of the use and influence of a tradition that, although lost to the professional theatre, has persisted in school and university.

FLATTER, RICHARD. *Shakespeare's Producing Hand: A Study of his Marks of Expression to be found in the First Folio*. Heinemann, 1948.

Based on the theory that the punctuation of the Folio is a deliberate guide to the performance of the plays.

GILDER, ROSAMOND. *John Gielgud's Hamlet*. Methuen, 1937.

A detailed record, with Gielgud's own notes on "The Hamlet Tradition".

JOSEPH, B. L. *Elizabethan Acting*. Oxford University Press, 1951. 12s. 6d.

A new approach through the parallel art of oratory.

LAVER, JAMES. *Drama: Its Costume and Décor*. Studio, 1951. 30s.

An historical study which discusses the theatre's relationship with other arts, deals particularly with the Baroque period and has over 200 excellent illustrations.

REYNOLDS, GEORGE FULLMER. *The Staging of Elizabethan Plays at the Red Bull Theatre*, 1605–1625. New York, M.L.A.A.; Oxford University Press, 1940.

A closely reasoned synthesis based on the known repertoire of the theatre.

SIMONSON, LEE. *The Art of Scenic Design: A Pictorial Analysis of Stage Setting and its relation to Theatrical Production*. Harrap, 1951. 35s.

SOUTHERN, RICHARD. *The Open Stage and the Modern Theatre in Research and Practice*. Faber, 1953. 12s. 6d.

The neo-Elizabethan reaction against the "picture-frame" stage.

Changeable Scenery: Its Origin and Development in the British Theatre. Faber, 1952. 63s.

A major study of much wider scope than the title suggests.

SPRAGUE, ARTHUR COLBY. *Shakespeare and the Actors: The Stage Business in his Plays* (1660–1905). Harvard University Press; Oxford University Press. 1944. 40s.

Shakespearian Players and Performances. Black, 1954. 15s.

Includes Betterton as Hamlet; Garrick as Lear; Kemble as Hamlet; Siddons as Lady Macbeth; Kean as Othello; Macready as Macbeth; Irving as Shylock; Booth as Iago; and has a chapter on Poel.

WATKINS, RONALD. *On Producing Shakespeare.* Joseph, 1950. 21s.

The author's productions at Harrow School have provided the most successful of experiments in the Poel tradition. For a detailed study of *A Midsummer-Night's Dream,* see the same author's *Moonlight at the Globe.*

WILLIAMS, RAYMOND. *Drama in Performance.* Muller, 1954. 8s. 6d.

An historical survey of methods of staging.

REFERENCE

BRITISH DRAMA LEAGUE. *The Player's Library: the Catalogue of the Library of the British Drama League.* Faber, 1950. 30s.; First Supplement, 1951, 8s. 6d.; Second Supplement 1954, 21s.

Mainly concerned with listing plays, but also includes many hundreds of books on the theatre.

BROWN, IVOR. *Theatre,* 1954–55. Reinhardt, 1955 (forthcoming). 18s.

Planned as the first of a series which will review the year's theatrical events and trends.

HARTNOLL, PHYLLIS (Editor). *The Oxford Companion to the Theatre.* Oxford University Press. 1952. 42s.

An unequal work, but the best is very good and some of the subjects dealt with will be sought in vain elsewhere.

LOWENBERG, ALFRED. *The Theatre of the British Isles, excluding London: A Bibliography.* Society for Theatre Research (issued to members only).

A thorough and very useful list of books and articles on the provincial theatres up to 1949.

LOWE, ROBERT W. *A Bibliographical Account of English Theatrical Literature from the Earliest Times to the Present Day* (1888). Nimmo, 1888.

This excellent reference book would normally be inaccessible to the general reader but it is included because a new edition, revised and extended to 1900, is in preparation under the auspices of the Society for Theatre Research.

PARKER, JOHN (Editor). *Who's Who in the Theatre: A Biographical Record of the Contemporary Stage.* Pitman, eleventh edition revised, 1952. 80s.

The latest edition of this invaluable record, which includes, as well as biographies of all well-known living personalities of the theatre, much other information, including genealogical tables, obituaries, dates of notable productions, etc.

STEPHENS, FRANCES (Editor). *Theatre World Annual (London): A Pictorial Review of West End Productions with a Record of Plays and Players.* Rockliff, Nos. 1–5, 1950–54 (in progress). 18s. each.

In each volume the year covers June–May.

"The Stage" Year Book, 1949–55 (in progress). The Stage. 10s. 6d. (1955 issue).

Each volume records the previous year's work in the theatre, with full casts of all important productions. An earlier series was published 1908–38.

Index of Authors

26

27

.

Lightning Source UK Ltd.
Milton Keynes UK
UKHW020928200721
387455UK00006B/288

9 781107 475151